S0-BUB-877

BOMBUS
Finds A Friend

Written by

Elsie Larson

Illustrations by

Elizabeth Haidle

DEDICATIONS

To Gail Denham
A good friend who has helped me to be a better friend.
— EJL

To the first friends I made in Savannah:
Amanda, Fay, Mark, Steve, Selena, and Chris —
Without whom this city would not feel like home.
— EH

BOMBUS FINDS A FRIEND
First Printing: May 1998

© 1998 Elsie Larson
Illustrations © Elizabeth Haidle
Art Design by Paul Haidle

All rights reserved.
No part of this book may be used or reproduced in any manner
whatsoever without written permission of the publisher, except
in the case of brief quotations in articles and reviews.
For information write:
Master Books, P.O. Box 727, Green Forest, AR 72638
ISBN: 0-89051-231-0
Library of Congress: 98:66307

Printed in the United States of America.

PREFACE

One day an experienced Sunday school teacher told me that many, many children in her classes confide that finding a friend is their most painful problem. Therefore, in this second Bombus story, I chose to write about the virtue of being a good friend.

When I was a child, I learned wisdom from animal fables. I regretted, however, that many cultures portrayed a disagreeable Creator, who was moody, mischievous, and sometimes mean.

In my imagined animal world, children may see wonders of the real creation and glimpse the wisdom of the real Creator, the loving God revealed in the Bible.

While fables are not intended to teach facts, they do teach truth. For me, every true virtue comes from God; every proven science fact shows the awesomeness of God. Bombus fables illustrate biblical virtues. The facts at the end of the story reveal wonders of the Creator's creation.

It is my hope that with the fable as a springboard, parents and teachers may teach more by using *Fun Science Facts, A Talking Time, Creative Activities,* and *Bible Search* in the back of the book.

— EJL, Gresham, Oregon, 1998

Long ago, a young bumblebee named Bombus lived in a flower-filled meadow. Every day he drank his fill of nectar. He was so happy, he felt he needed nothing more, not even a friend.

One day a great wind snatched Bombus from
the highest hollyhock and carried him off above
the treetops. Through the air he tumbled like a fat,
furry seed pod. The wind blew him so fast it took
his breath away and made his eyes water.

When a leaf whipped by, he grabbed it with all six
feet and held on. Riding the leaf was no better, but he was
afraid to let go. At last the wind slowed to a breeze and the
leaf sailed toward the ground.

Below lay a strange meadow splashed with poppies,
dandelions, clover, daisies, and bachelor buttons,
but no hollyhocks. In the middle of the meadow
sparkled a lake and a wide stream.

Fanning his wings to a steady buzz, Bombus let go of the drifting leaf and flew toward the flowers.

Landing on clover, he exclaimed, "Where am I? How will I ever find my way home?"

A raspy voice answered, "That's your problem. Get off my clover!"

Bombus leaned over and looked down. A caterpillar glared up at him from a half-eaten leaf.

"Excuse me," said Bombus. "I didn't know this was yours. Can you tell me how to get back to my hollyhock garden?"

"Foolish hymenoptera!* (hi-ma-nop'-tar-a) Don't you know that all meadows and gardens belong to the Creator who sent the seeds and sun and rain?"

*insect with membranous wings.

The caterpillar grabbed a
mouthful of leaf, closed its
eyes, and chewed.
"A bumblebee's hollyhock
garden! Indeed!"

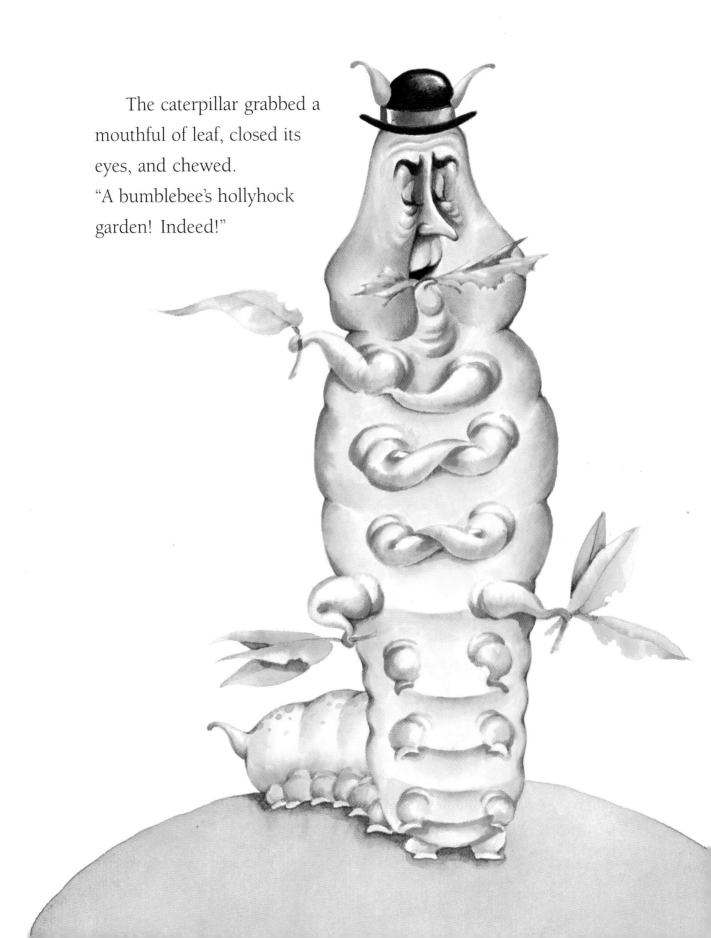

Bombus asked hopefully, "May I gather some nectar?"

"What? First you want to go home; now you want to eat," grumbled the caterpillar. "You should have my problem! When this clover is gone, I shall starve."

"But there's a lot of clover!" Bombus exclaimed.

"What? Where? Show me," said the caterpillar.

Bombus didn't want to stay and help such an unfriendly person. He said, "Just look around, and you'll see."

Bombus flew to some bachelor buttons. "Hello!" he called. "Is anybody living here?"

Someone squeaked, "Can't you see this is a Philaenus Spumarius* (phil-a'-nus spu-mar'-e-us) village?" Out of a nest of foamy bubbles popped the worried face of a small green bug.

More tiny bugs poked their heads out of their bubble houses and cried, "Don't bother us! We must finish our homes before the sun grows hot!"

*from scientific name for spittle bugs - Order Homoptera, Family Cercopidae, Genus Philaenus, species spumarius.

Bombus really needed a friend
so he bothered them anyway.
"Please tell me how to return
to my hollyhock garden."

A plump grandmother bug said, "If you must bumble around here, make yourself useful. Watch over our children."

"I don't know anything about bug child-sitting!"

"Then go away!" all the bugs cried.

A mischievous bug child blew a stream of bubbles at Bombus. The shiny globes wrapped around his leg. Shaking himself free, he quickly said goodbye.

Tired, hungry, and worried,
Bombus flew to the lake.

"Everyone is so unfriendly. I
wish I had a friend," he said.

He landed on the lip of a
snapdragon and snatched a drink.
No one yelled at him. He drank
from another. Still no one told him
no. Working from the top to the
bottom of the stalk, he drank his fill.

When he backed out of the last blossom, he came face to face
with a large, fierce insect, clinging to a cattail blade just above the
water. It waved its sharp pincer jaws at him.

"Oh, oh! H-h-hello," Bombus stammered.
"If these are your flowers, please excuse me.
I was so hungry."

The creature rubbed its pincers across its mouth. Bombus was afraid to move for fear the monster might snatch him. Suddenly the frightful thing swelled behind its head and split open. It was growing out of its shell. A glistening blue-green head with enormous eyes peeked from the scary brown shell.

The big-eyed head was followed by a slender body. It struggled until it hung upside down, half in and half out, limp and helpless.

Forgetting himself, Bombus cried, "Do you need help?"

The large eyes turned toward him. "No, thank you," it whispered. "I must do this by myself."

Stretching and stretching, the insect reached upward. Finally it caught hold of the leaf above its old shell and pulled its body free.

"Oh, you're beautiful!" Bombus exclaimed.

"Thank you. I am Doreena Dragonfly. Soon I shall be able to fly."

"I can fly, too," said Bombus. He took off, circled the cattail, and landed expertly on a leaf beside her. "But I can't see your wings." he said.

Doreena wriggled short stubs on her back. "First I must inflate my wings. That is the way of dragonflies. I hope a frog or turtle or fish does not catch me, resting here so close to the water."

As Bombus watched, her crumpled wings slowly unfolded. He glanced down at the water. "Climb higher!" he exclaimed.

"I can't! I'm not strong enough yet!"

Then from the water below her, a frog
hopped onto a lily pad.

"Look out!" Bombus yelled. He zoomed
down and hit the frog's nose. The startled frog
dived off the pad and swam away.

After that, Bombus flew around and
around Doreena. When underwater
creatures approached,
he chased them away.

Finally, she said, "Thank you. Now I can fly!" Away she flew before he could even say goodbye.

Bombus said, "Well, no one so beautiful and fast would be my friend. Oh, how will I ever find my way home?"

"But I am your friend." Doreena hovered above, like a hummingbird.

Bombus looked at her long shimmering wings. "I could never keep up with you."

"I can fly fast or slow. Where would you like to go?"

Bombus told her about the great wind that had carried him
so far from his own meadow. "I want to go home," he said.

"I can fly like the wind," she said. "I will carry you back
home." She clasped him with her six legs and away they went.

Bombus blinked wind-tears from his eyes and watched
the earth below. At last he called, "There it is!"

Doreena flew down and placed him on a hollyhock.

"Thank you," he said

"You're welcome. Now I must return to my home."

"Will you come back to visit?"

"Oh, yes. You helped me, and a dragonfly never forgets a friend." Away she flew.

"Neither does a bumblebee!" he shouted after her.

"What a good friend she is," said Bombus.
"Maybe the bug family and caterpillar would
have been friends, too, if I had helped them."

"What's all that noise?" grouched
an unfriendly voice.

Bombus looked down and saw a frowning katydid. Nodding politely, Bombus said, "Good day, Mr. Katydid. Is there anything I can do to HELP you, sir?"

"Might be," said Mr. Katydid, and on his face in place of the frown, curved a friendly katydid smile.

The End

fun facts about
dragonflies

Among the most beautiful of insects, dragonflies come in many bright body colors, such as crimson, blue, and green. In the sunshine, their transparent wings flash colors of the rainbow.

Considered one of our most helpful insects, each one patrols a regular route, gobbling up hundreds of mosquitoes before they bite us. Dragonflies are fun to watch. They do not sting. If you caught one, however, it could bite with its strong pincer jaws.

The large eyes of the dragonfly contain 28,000 lenses which can see to the right, to the left, up, down, ahead, and even behind, without a turn of the body or head.

In flight, dragonflies beat their wings 25 to 40 times per second while bumblebees and flies make 200 wing-beats per second. Yet in one second a dragonfly can travel 45 feet or more. Some dragonflies have been clocked at 60 miles per hour. (A 60-miles-per-hour wind can topple trees.) This speedy flier can stop instantly, fly backward, and hover like a helicopter.

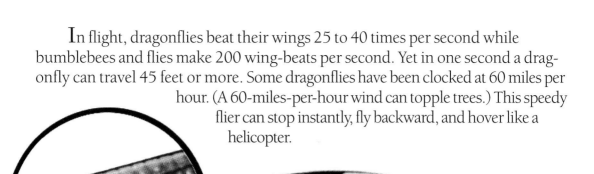

Unlike most flying insects, its pairs of wings are unlinked, so they flap independently. For hovering, the front pair creates a downbeat, while the second pair makes an upbeat. This X-shaped movement allows a dragonfly to hang in the air as if suspended on an invisible string.

Some dragonflies are very large. In Australia, the petalura has a wingspan of 7 inches. In North America, the green darner reaches a 5 to 6 inch wingspan. Fossils have been found of dragonflies with wingspans of 29 inches. Do you wonder how big mosquitoes were in those days?

If you want to puzzle someone, ask: what has six legs, but cannot walk?

The answer: a dragonfly. It uses its legs only for catching food and occasionally to perch.

Dragonflies spend their lives in flight. Their six spiny legs, at the front of their long bodies, make good nets for catching dinner. At 25 miles per hour, they catch and eat mosquitoes and flies.

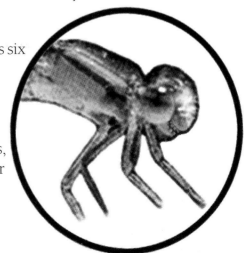

a talking time

What made Doreena believe that Bombus was her friend?

What could Bombus have done to be a friend to the caterpillar?

What could Bombus have done to be a friend to the little bugs?

Do you know an unfriendly person?
What do they do (or not do) to make you feel they are unfriendly?

What shows you that a person wants to be friends?

Have you ever needed a friend to help you?
   When? What happened?

What can you do when you need a friend?
   Bombus would say, "To make a friend, be a friend."
   (Sadly, this is also a time to discuss the danger of *accepting
   friendly offers* from a strange adult.)

Name some of your friends.
   Why do you like them?
   What makes a good friend?
   Why are friends important?

Some friends are grownups who help you. Name some.
(Examples: parents, grandparents, teachers in Sunday School and school,
   pastors, firefighters, paramedics, police, other community servants.)

What are some of the things you wish a friend would do for you?
What can you do to be a better friend?

creative activities

Chosen to remind us that a good friendship depends upon
caring about others, taking turns, and letting others be first.

A BOMBUS PARTY — a way to help a new friend get acquainted.
Host child may prepare a gift certificate for each guest to take home at the
end of the party, promising to be a good helper when one is needed.
Foods:
Nectar — provide different colors of fruit juice or fruit-flavored drinks.
Flower garden muffins or cupcakes: push a piece of plastic drinking straw
into the top. Just before serving, tuck a flower blossom into the straw.
(Nasturtiums and squash blossoms are edible.)
Begin the party by reading: *Bombus Finds a Friend*

Suggested Games:
"Bombus Home Search"
Children hunt for flower pictures hidden in the room.
The one who finds the hollyhock wins *Doreena's Helpful Friend Award*
(a green ribbon badge to wear throughout the party).

"Stick the Bumblebee on the Flower"
Make a poster of painted flowers or pictures of flowers cut out from a
garden catalog. Place the largest flower in the center for a "target."
Draw a bumblebee on a "sticky" note paper. Color it and cut it out, leaving
on enough sticky paper so children can take turns being blindfolded and sticking
the bee on the poster.

"Bombus Musical Chair"
For music, play "The Flight of the Bumblebee." Under the seat of one chair
tape a paper bumblebee. The child who sits on the Bombus chair gives her seat
to the child who is left standing. Do not remove any chairs for this game.
The winner is the one who most often lands on the Bombus chair, which
she gives to the child who has none. Prize: a blue ribbon to wear, marked
Good Friend of the Day.

"Make a Treat for a Friend"
(To take home as a thank you for someone.) Children decorate cookies with
frosting, raisins, candy bits, shredded coconut, pretzel pieces, or colored boxed
cereals to make a bee, ladybug, beetle, or imaginary insect. (Make two and eat one.)

For an Outdoor Party:

Provide each child with small magnifying glasses for observing insects.

Collect wildflowers. Place them between sheets of wax paper to be pressed later in a book. Parent or teacher may seal the edges of the paper with a warm iron for carrying home.

Explain: When the flowers are dried, the child can glue them to art paper to make a picture or a greeting card for a friend. Tip: have a finished dried flower gift to show.

OTHER ACTIVITIES:

Learn more about insects —

Visit a zoo that maintains an insect collection.

Look in books: find out how many varieties of insects have been identified.
Are insects valuable to animals? to plants? to people?

Write about one interesting insect and draw its picture.

Handcraft — A Pretty Paper Weight for a Friend
You will need:

A small pickle or jelly jar
A piece of lumber (about 4″ by 4″ by 1″)
Craft jewelry glue
Craft gemstones
Small silk flowers
3″ length of tinsel rope (iridescent white)
Acrylic black paint for wood
Metallic gold paint for metal jar lid
A craft paintbrush for each paint
Optional: rick-rack to match flower colors and/or a small chenille bumblebee

Directions: Paint the wood black. Paint the jar lid gold.

Glue gemstones to the bottom of the pickle jar. (The bottom will become the top, so make it pretty.) Place flowers in pickle jar, upside-down and facing the sides of the jar. (Optional — place bumblebee on a flower.)

Tuck the tinsel in the top of the jar. Screw lid onto the jar. Turn the jar upside-down. Glue the top of the lid to the center of the black wood for a base. (Optional — glue rick-rack around the edge of the wood and/or glue more gemstones on the black base.)

bible search

Why should we offer to help someone in need?
Read what Jesus says in Luke 6:35-36 and Mark 12:28-31.

Who is my friend? Read what Jesus says in Luke 10:29-37.
    (Would Jesus want us to treat friends as He wants us to treat neighbors?)

Read James 1:22-25. Would a person who did this be a good friend?

Why is it important to be a good friend?
    Read what Jesus says in John 13:34-35.

Read about a prince who chose friendship over becoming a king:
    1 Samuel, chapter 20.

Read Proverbs 17:17. What does it mean?
    Write this wise saying on a bookmark or make a poster or wall plaque to remind yourself to be a good friend.

How did God prepare the earth for bumblebees, dragonflies, and other insects?
Read Genesis 1:11 and 1:30. How does God care for insects today?

Read about insect behavior in science books:
    How do bees learn how to build nests, comunicate with each other, and make honey?
    After living underwater most of its life, how does a dragonfly know how to fly backward or what to eat or how to catch insects in the air?

Read about some of God's amazing designs for animals in Job 39, 40, and 41.

What other questions come to your mind?
Search for answers!

Look for

The First Bombus Picture Book Story

BOMBUS THE BUMBLEBEE
Written by Elsie Larson
Illustrated by David Haidle & Elizabeth Haidle

When the honeybees tease Bombus, telling him he's too fat to fly, he loses confidence. He tries to fly like other insects and only proves to himself the honeybees are right. He isn't shaped right for flying. The happy ending for Bombus cheers kids who may have felt unattractive or different.

In the non-fiction section at the back of the book, kids from three to ninety-three will be amazed at the science facts about bumblebees.

"Talking Time" contains suggestions to help parents or teachers discuss with children diversity, teasing, and peer pressure.

"Creative Activities" strengthen the message of the fable as well as add to the fun of the book.

"Ideas from Parents of Confident Kids" and "Bible Search" round out the multiple ways to use this original Bombus fable.

Look also for
A BOMBUS CREATIVITY BOOK
40 pages of creative activities to enhance the storybooks